THE GRAPHIC ART
ENAMEL BA

'THE ERROR IS SUPERIOR TO THE CRAFTSMANSHIP'

(seen on an old carpenter's signboard, Syros, Greece)

THE GRAPHIC ART OF THE
ENAMEL BADGE

Ken Sequin

With 581 colour illustrations

THAMES AND HUDSON

All badges have been proportionally enlarged by 270% (with the exception of those illustrated in the introduction and those marked with an asterisk in the list of illustrations).

Loaned badges
213, 222, 224, 226, 227, 398, 499, 500, 515, 558 (Leo Lonergan); 402 (Russell Field)

Illustrations © 1999 Ken Sequin
Text © 1999 Ken Sequin

British Library Cataloguing-in-Publication Data

A catalogue record for this book is available from the British Library

ISBN 0-500-28121-1

Printed and bound in Hong Kong

On the cover:
FRONT, top row, from left to right,
Late R.M.S. *Titanic* April 15th 1912, Jaguar Coventry, Scott's Jams, Guinness is Good for You, The Old Covered Bridge. *Bottom row, from left to right,* National Asylum Workers' Union, Hoover Derby & Perivale, Windsor Water Woollies, Daily Express Rupert League.

BACK, from top to bottom,
ZIP Guaranteed Oils, The Lambeth Walk, Father William.

Frontispiece:
T.A. Established 1849
F.S.
Membership badge of the Typographical Association made by Fattorini and Sons.

CONTENTS

T he earliest known badges originate from the 12th century when the Pope granted the authorities in Rome the right to make and market pewter badges adorned with images of St Peter and St Paul. They could be purchased as a sign of devotion, while also providing pilgrims with proof that they had made a pilgrimage to a shrine – pilgrims often travelled vast distances and were sponsored by townspeople and villagers who were unable to make the journey themselves. During the Middle Ages, many shrines throughout Christendom became places of pilgrimage. In 1392, a shrine in Munich, Germany, received over 40,000 visitors, four times the city's population at the time. Several badges dating from this period have been found on riverbanks, including the banks of the Thames near the site of the legendary Tarbard Inn at Southwark, where, according to Chaucer, pilgrims gathered on their way to Canterbury. Perhaps badges, like coins, were thrown into the water for good luck as in present-day Rome.

In Britain in the last years of the 18th century the Quakers were waging a war against the slave trade and the Quaker firm of Wedgwood issued a ceramic medallion denouncing the trade. In 1807 William Wilberforce ordered 50,000 medallions, emblazoned with an anti-slavery motto, to be made by Edward Thompson of Birmingham. Wilberforce was a prominent figure in the Anti-Slavery Movement and also the incumbent MP for Hull – he ordered the medallions

The Thames Guild of Free Watermen
Thames watermen were essentially river taxi drivers. The guild, established in 1555, regulated the watermen and implemented a fair pricing system. The badge illustrated is from the late 18th century and would have been worn on the sleeve (probably of a leather jerkin) attached through the holes at either side. (113mm wide)

in an attempt to defend his parliamentary seat. This expanded parliamentary suffrage and was one of the first parliamentary campaigns. His political opponents, Viscount Lascelles and Lord Milton, responded by ordering medallions from the same source. Wilberforce won by a substantial majority and retained his seat.

In America clothing buttons depicting George Washington were produced when he was running for President in 1789. However, it was not until the election of Andrew Jackson in 1824 that America saw a similar badge war.

In Britain during the 1840s the advent of die-stamping technology in the industrial Midlands made the production of metal badges cheaper. Clubs, societies, trade unions and charitable concerns swiftly recognized the enormous potential of lapel badges as propaganda, and cheerful and colourful enamel badges were soon seen on jacket lapels up and down the country.

In Britain badges were also used by the guilds – associations of craftsmen or merchants – to identify their members. For example, the Thames Guild of Free Watermen, who plied goods and passengers up and down the Thames, wore large imposing arm badges attached to their jerkins by leather thongs. These badges identified them as bona fide licensed watermen.

In the early 19th century philanthropic institutions found badges useful in identifying both officials and recipients of charitable concerns. Causes such as

temperance were prominent in the developing industrial centres in America and Britain and those pledging to abstain from drink were asked to wear a badge to encourage others to join the cause.

The design of most 19th-century British badges mimicked the sedate ornate and heraldic steel-engraved emblems of the time. However, established jewellers such as the firms of Thomas Fattorini and Fattorini and Sons (two rival firms from the same family) used innovative designs, stamping their authority on the industry. They employed Art Nouveau and other fashionable styles, examples of which can be seen in their sample catalogues. Worth particular attention is

Band of Hope
Established in 1854, the Band of Hope Union issued several 'pledge' badges. (actual size)

7

the work of William Miller, a former employee of Thomas Fattorini. During the early 1920s he established a rival firm in Birmingham which produced delicate cut-out figural badges with rich and colourful enamelling, often with contrasting transparent and opaque enamels which included relief moulding below the enamelled surface, lending realism to the badges' design. During the inter-war period Strattons, also of Birmingham, and Gaunt of London were major manufacturers.

Initially, the production of badges was concentrated in Bradford and Birmingham, spreading out from there to industrial centres all over Europe – Paris and Milan were the most prominent. In America, although enamel badges were not produced, there was a far greater demand for tintype, ferrotype and subsequently button badges – the latter were easier and cheaper to produce and have continued to dominate the American market.

The Boys' Home Regent's Park
This richly patinated 19th-century cap badge incorporates the beehive motif, signifying industrious endeavour. (actual size)

Britain Rules
A patriotic emblem emblazoned on a silver badge produced at the outbreak of World War I. (actual size)

Faithful Unto Death
Numerous mementoes were produced in 1884 when the heroic death of General Gordon at Khartoum was reported. Recently it has been revealed that the government, wishing to play down the defeat at Khartoum, falsified accounts of the event. Gordon had in fact been taken prisoner and died in captivity because the government had delayed payment of the ransom demanded for his release. (actual size)

Enamel badges were an important form of propaganda during World War I, exhorting the population to work even harder for victory. And over the two decades after the end of the war badges became part of all areas of social and cultural life.

As well as advertising collective beliefs and desires, badges often serve as attractive items of jewelry. They are particularly appealing to children and advertisers set out to make their badges as attractive as possible to encourage children to collect them. The following quotation is from a manufacturer's trade catalogue of 1939: 'Children are by nature badge wearers and will carry your message for you everywhere. A few thousand of these inexpensive badges distributed to children will more than repay your outlay.'

During the 1920s national and provincial newspapers began to feature children's corners which issued a wide variety of membership badges. Child mortality had risen because of diphtheria and other diseases and the money raised from the badges was used to fund much-needed cots in children's wards up and down the country. Children's radio circles also flourished. They were usually fronted by a spurious uncle or auntie, the most famous of which was Uncle Mac (in reality Dennis McCullah), who hosted BBC Children's Hour. The badges, although long redundant, now turn up at antique fairs where they are snapped up by collectors trying to complete a set.

During World War II shortages of raw materials curtailed all but the 'Homefront' from issuing badges, and although production flourished after the hostilities ceased, synthetic materials began to replace the rich vitreous enamels of the pre-war era, producing a more uniform and less tactile badge. As plastic began to replace the base metal, many firms folded or were bought out by the larger firms such as Fattorini. Sadly, Millers closed in the late 1960s, leaving very few manufacturers of vitreous enamel badges in business today.

The Statesman Benji League
A comic strip character popular in this Indian newspaper in the 1930s. (actual size)

12

9

10

11

BLANCHE

P. C.
S MILK
GUARDIAN
OF
HEALTH

HATS
&
BOOTS
JACKSONS

12

13

14

MELTONIAN

SAUCY BUT QUITE
'O.K'

LE CŒUR SUR LA MAIN
BENJAMIN

15

16

17

13

18

19

20

21

22

23

24

25

26

32

33

34

35

43

44

45

46

47

48

49

50

55   56   57   58   59

SONNY SUNGLOW

60

61

62

63

65

64

66

67

25

68

69

70

71

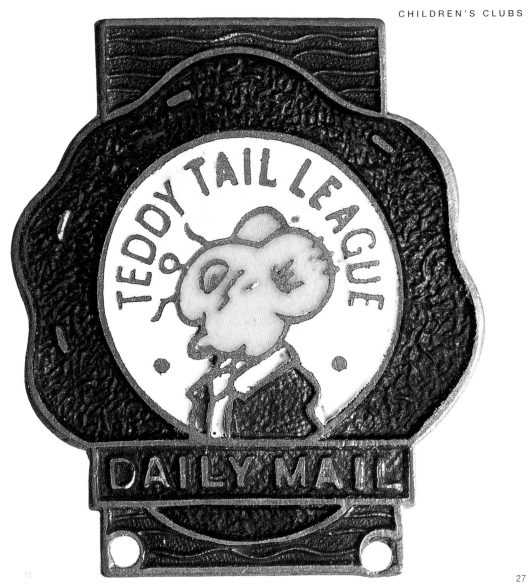

73

74

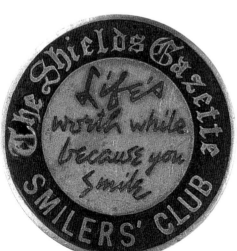

75

76

77

78

79

80

81

82

83

90

91

92

93

94

102

103

104

105

35

106

107

108

109

110

111

112

113

114

115

116

117

119

GEO WEST

120

MONA
VIVIAN

118

121

DOODLES

122

123

124

125

126

127

128

129

130

131

132

133

134

S. B. CLUB

141

THREE OF US

142

GAY LIEUTENANT

143

CAROLINA MOON

144

145

44

146

147

THE LAMBETH WALK

THE LAMBETH WALK

148

149

BY THE OLD
FASHIONED MILL

150

151

LIGHTS OUT

45

158

159

160

161

162

163

164

MELVIN

SILVRY MOON

THE BRIDAL WALTZ

CALL ME SWEETHEART

QUEEN MARY

QUEEN OF THE SEA

165

166

167

168

169

170

171

172

173

174

175

176

177

49

178

179

180

181

182

183

STILL UPWARD

28TH·NATIONAL CONVENTION· CE BRISTOL 1920·

184

SALVATION ARMY

185

PERFORMING & CAPTIVE ANIMALS DEFENCE LEAGUE
JUSTICE
LIBERTY
JACK LONDON CLUB

186

FOR EXCEPTIONAL
ATTENDANCE
PRESENTED
BY THE
SUNDAY
SCHOOL
UNION

187

PILOTS
C.U. & L.M.S

188

PROV.III.17

189

53

190

191

192

193

194

195

204

205

206

212

213

214

215

60

216

217

218

219

220

221

222

223

WOMEN'S SUFFRAGE.

LEAGUE OF EMPIRE · HOUSEWIVES

BUY EMPIRE GOODS

· ANTI GERMAN UNION 1916 ·
GOOD QUEEN BESS EXPELLED ALL GERMANS
BRITAIN FOR THE BRITISH
1597

BOYCOTT GERMAN
BUY BRITISH
GOODS

230

231

*For further trade union badges, see the sections
on Maritime, Motoring, and Railways & Trams
in the chapter on travel*

235

236

237

238

HACKNEY & KINGSLAND COSTERS & TRADERS UNION.

239

LIVERPOOL · COOPERS · SOCIETY

240

WIGAN & DIST WEAVERS. WINDERS ETC. ASSN

241

AMALGAMATED UNION OF OPERATIVE BAKERS & CONFECTIONERS

242

243

244

245

246

247

248

249

250

251

252

253

254

255

256

257

258

259

260

261

262

263

264

265

266

267

268

269

270

271

272

273

274

275

276

277

278

279

281

282

280

284

283

285

286

287

288

289

290

291

292

293

294

300

301

302

303

304

305

306

307

308

309

310

311

312

313

314

315

SHEFFIELD SPEEDWAY
SUPPORTERS' CLUB

316

317

318

319

320

321

322

323

324

325

326

327

328

POLLARDS HASKINS M-S-C
ABOVE
POLLARDS
AIRCRAFT

329

G·A·S·C

330

PIONEERS
EN AVANT

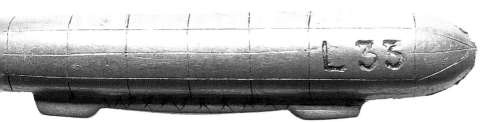

331

332

333

334

335

336

337

338

339

340

341

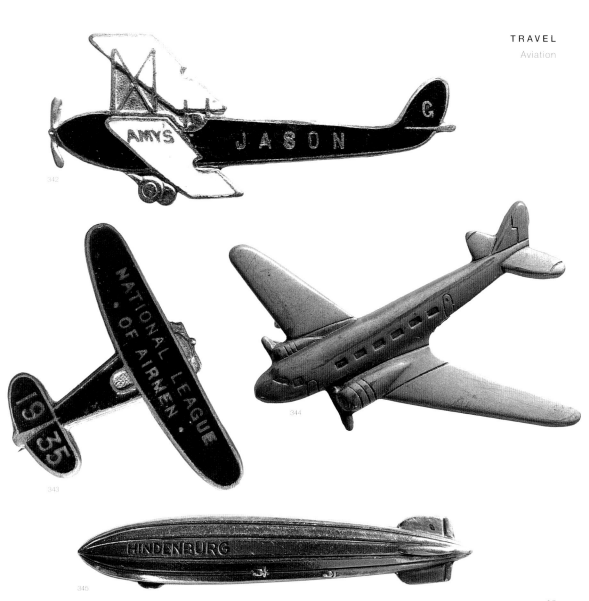

342

343

344

345

346

347

348

349

350

351

352

353

354

355

356

357

358

359

360

361

99

366

367

368

369

370

101

371

372

373

374

375

376

377

378

379

380

381

382

383

105

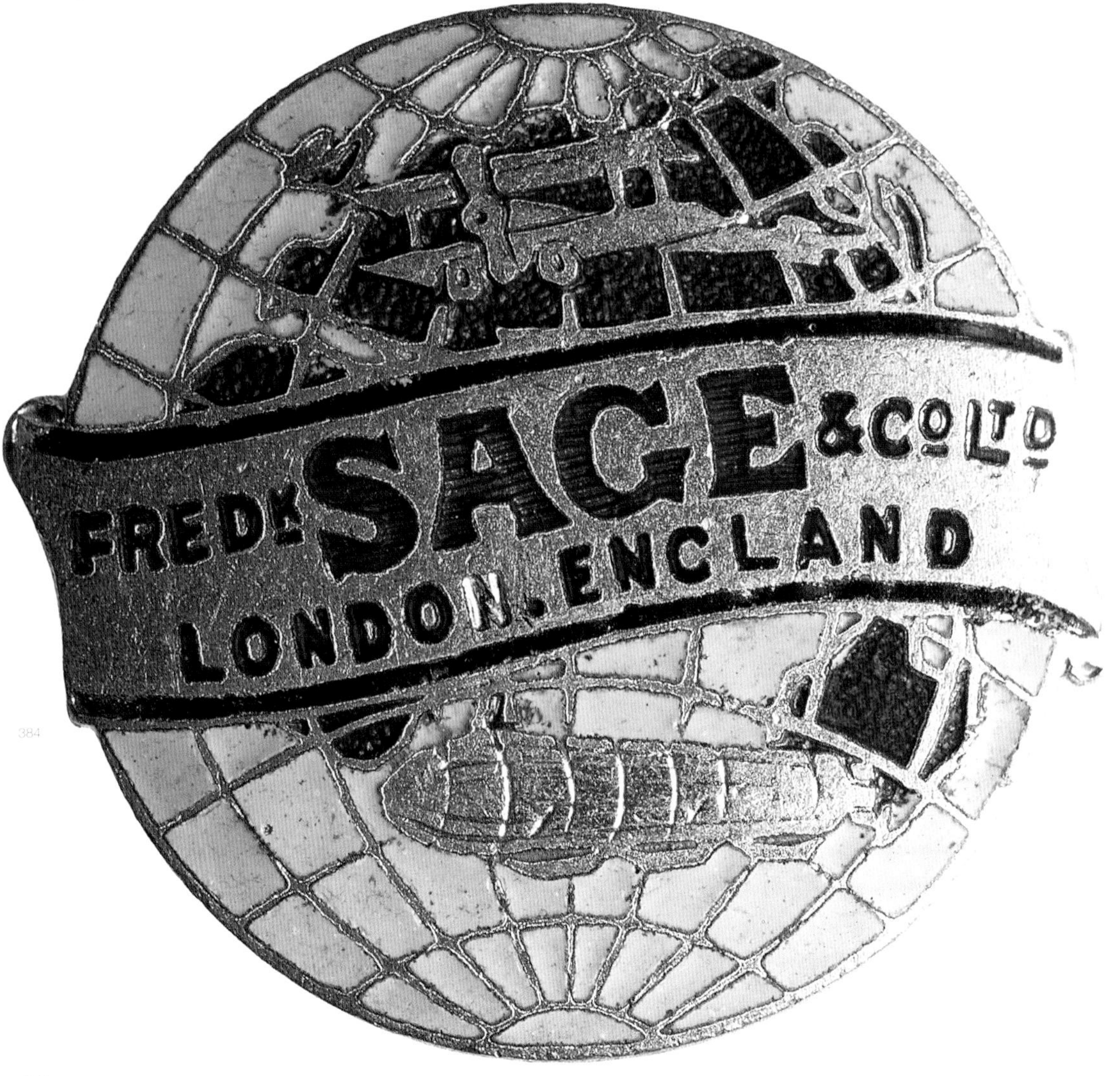

384

385

386

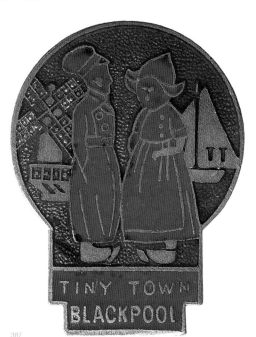

387

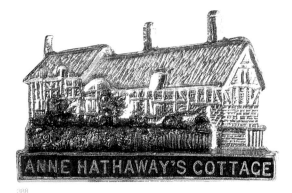

388

389

390

391

109

R.M.S. CORSICAN.

401

402

403

404

405

406

407–418

419

420

421

422

423

424

117

N. A. S. & D.

DOCKERS SECTION

425

N.U.S.

ANNUAL GENERAL MEETING

N.U.S.

LONDON 1931

426

NATIONAL UNION OF GENERAL & MUNICIPAL WORKERS

FISH 1 BOBBER

427

N. U. OF D. L.

428

429

430

431

119

432

433

434

435

436

437

438

439

441

440

442

443

444

445

446

447

448

449

450

451

452

453

USE DRACONFLY MOTOR OILS AND GREASES

454

455

456

457

458

459

460

461

462

463

464

465

466

467

468

469

470

471

472

473

474

475

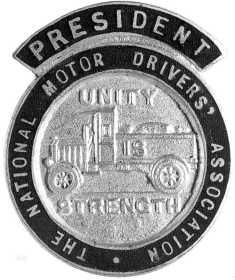

476

129

477

478

479

480

481

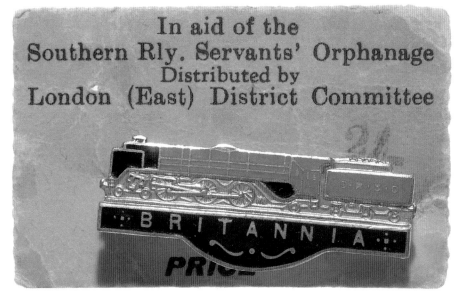

485

486

487

488

489

490

491

490

497

498

499

500

501

502

503

504

505

506

507

508

АВРОРА

ALL CLEAR

SOLDIERS
AND SAILORS
BLINDED IN
THE WAR
St DUNSTAN'S
STANDS FOR
VICTORY OVER
BLINDNESS

509

510

511

512

513

514

515

THE WAR YEARS

Homefront (1939–1945)

516

517

518

519

520

521

522

523

524

525

526

527

144

528

529

530

531

532

533

534

535

536

537

538

539

540

542

541

543

SPIT

FIRE

BOMBER CLUB

ST PANCRAS

544

545

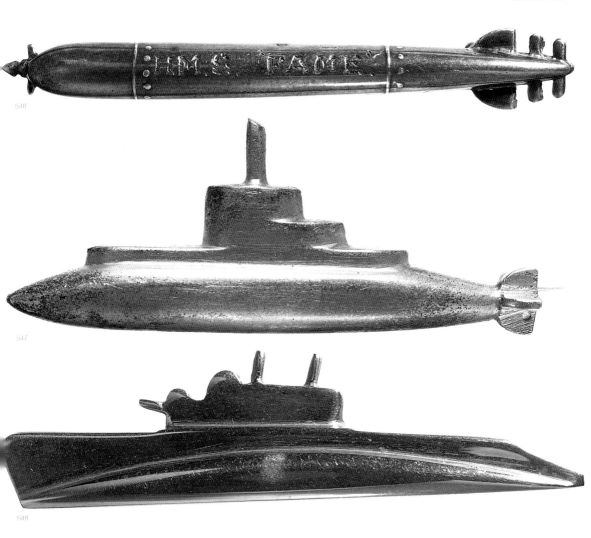

546

547

548

549

550

551

552

553

554

555

556

557

558

559

560

561

562

563

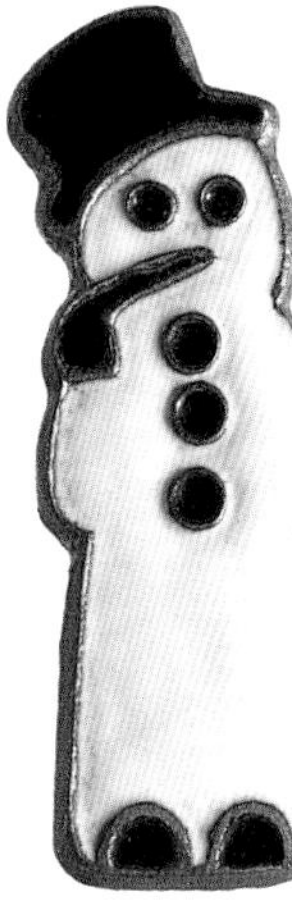

564

565

566

567

568

569

570

571

572

573

574

The present interest in material culture often leads to artefacts acquiring a monetary value which they did not previously have, prompting antique dealers to seek them out. Most general dealers in small collectibles now carry the odd badge or two. Occasionally, specialist badge dealers can be found at antique collectors' fairs and in established street markets, notwithstanding the almost ubiquitous antique arcades in many market towns.

In Britain several badge collectors' clubs have been established, some of which are highly specialized. Their magazines have an editorial content and carry advertisements offering badges for sale and listing those wanted by members.

In America, although enamel badges are manufactured, button badges are far more common and, together with earlier tintypes, are widely collected. Political campaign examples are especially in demand.

Care and Display

Old enamel badges often survive in excellent condition – perhaps because they have been popped into a drawer and forgotten, possibly being considered too attractive an item to discard completely.

If a badge requires cleaning or renovating it should be undertaken with care and with due regard for its natural ageing and for any normal wear and tear that may have occurred over the years. When a badge has lost its original gilt, it can often take on a softer and less raw appearance, especially if it has darkened and acquired an attractive patina.

Normally all you will need to do is briefly immerse it in a saucer of lemon juice to loosen any grime and then give it a quick rinse under running water while gently scrubbing it with a soft brush. The appearance of an over-cleaned and too highly polished badge can be aesthetically revolting. Similarly, any significant repairs attempted on the enamel can be potentially disastrous. The easy availability of modellers' enamel paints can result in the vandalization of otherwise attractively aged, although chipped, badges. Colours can be easily matched, but transparent colours placed over an uncleaned base metal can significantly alter their intended appearance. Unless undertaken with care, you should refrain from such unpredictable restoration work.

Broken or missing fastenings can be replaced, but there is a case for leaving the badge as it is, in order to retain its authenticity.

If you want to display your badges there are various options. You can use glazed display frames, but they can be very expensive, perhaps exceeding the original cost of the badges and it makes close examination of them difficult. Deeply recessed coin cases are even more expensive, but are a practical alternative. Inexpensive plastic boxes produced for cigarette-card collectors can work just as well, depending on your requirements, and will only mean a modest outlay.

Dating Badges

The most widely encountered manufacturers of badges
are Thomas Fattorini and Fattorini and Sons. They
were from the same family, but in the 19th century they
formed separate companies, although they re-grouped
in 1986. Their locations were as follows.

Thomas Fattorini

1827–1919	Birmingham
1886–1934	Skipton
1916–1927	Hockley St, Birmingham
1919–1927	Bolton
1927–1986	Regent St, Birmingham

Fattorini and Sons

1613–1916	Bradford
1916–1986	Barr St, Birmingham

The numbering sequence of British Registered Designs
began in 1884. The table below should aid the dating
of badges that have a registration number. Although
registration of American patents began in 1836, I have
not encountered American enamel badges which
display a registration number.

1	1884	630,190	1914
20,000	1885	644,935	1915
40,800	1886	653,521	1916
64,700	1887	658,980	1917
81,800	1888	662,872	1918
117,800	1889	666,128	1919
142,300	1890	673,750	1920
164,000	1891	680,147	1921
186,400	1892	687,144	1922
206,100	1893	694,999	1923
225,000	1894	702,671	1924
248,200	1895	710,165	1925
268,800	1896	718,057	1926
291,400	1897	726,330	1927
311,677	1898	734,370	1928
332,200	1899	740,725	1929
351,600	1900	751,160	1930
368,186	1901	760,583	1931
385,180	1902	769,670	1932
403,200	1903	779,292	1933
424,400	1904	789,019	1934
447,800	1905	799,097	1935
471,860	1906	808,794	1936
493,900	1907	817,293	1937
518,640	1908	825,231	1938
535,170	1909	832,610	1939
575,817 *	1910	837,520	1940
594,195	1912		
612,431	1913	*same prefix for 1911	

LIST OF ILLUSTRATIONS

the first in a long line of children's puppets on British TV.

101
Hull Times Children's Club
T.F. LTD BIRMINGHAM
The full title should be the Hull Times Merrytimers' Club.

102
Uncle Jack's Cheerio Club
Bristol Times & Mirror
THOMAS FATTORINI
HOCKLEY ST BIRMINGHAM

103
Girl Adventurers
This was one of several comics published by the Hulton Press during the 1950s.

104
League of Youth
T.F. BIRMINGHAM
DAILY SKETCH AND SUNDAY
GRAPHIC. THOMAS
FATTORINI LTD B'HAM
A design reminiscent of the resurgent medievalism of the Arts and Crafts Movement (c. 1920).

105
Spiv and Let Spiv
The Spiv's image as a flashily attired small-time racketeer was enshrined by the *Spivs Union*, a satirical journal published in the mid-1940s. This is the journal's spoof club badge.

106–113 [107*]
Untitled
This remarkable group of badges was discovered in an Athens market. They appear to depict types of acts popular in pre-1940s Paris at such venues as the Comedie Française. There are no maker's marks, but they are almost certainly continental in origin.

114
Lester's Midgets
W.MILLER 118 BRANSTON ST B'HAM REG 732142
A theatrical troupe.

115*
Untitled
An unusual child entertainer. 'No 24' appears on the reverse of the badge and may indicate that this was part of a series.

116
H.M.S. Lilliput Ropers Midgets
W.MILLER LTD
118 BRANSTON ST B'HAM REGD 784019
Harry Roper's troupe toured extensively throughout Europe during the 1920s and 1930s.

117
Fiery Jack
Resident clown of Blackpool Tower's Circus.

118*
Mona Vivian
H.W.M.
Acrobatic star of Blackpool Tower's Circus.

119
Geo West
H.W.MILLER LTD BRANSTON ST B'HAM 18
Resident clown of Blackpool Tower's Circus.

120
Untitled
H.W.MILLER LTD BRANSTON ST B'HAM 18
An unidentified theatrical 'Dame'.

121
Doodles
H.W.MILLER LTD BRANSTON ST B'HAM 18
Doodles was the stage name of William McAliser – sky diver and resident clown at the Blackpool Tower during the 1920s and 1930s.

122
Doodles
H.W.MILLER LTD BRANSTON ST B'HAM COPYRIGHT
Here Doodles is shown with the Blackpool Tower.

123
6KH Radio Circle
THOMAS FATTORINI
HOCKLEY ST BIRMINGHAM
During the 1920s children could join their local radio station's children's circle and receive a badge displaying the

radio station's call sign. The correspondence generated enabled the station to evaluate the effectiveness of its transmitters.

124
BBC Radio Circle
MILLER
118 BRANSTON ST B'HAM
In 1930 the stations were reorganized and the badges became uniform, incorporating regional rather than city names.

125
Club des Petits Amis de Radio Cote D'Azur

126
Eddystone
The 'Rolls Royce' of short wave radios.

127
Bush
TOYE & CO LONDON

128
Associated Rediffusion Space Agent
A TV hire company.

129
Odeon Mickey Mouse Club
W.O. LEWIS BADGES
BIRMINGHAM
Only two years after Mickey Mouse's début in *Steamboat Willie* there were many hundreds of children's matinée clubs offering a staple diet of cartoons, serials and

features – and on both sides of the Atlantic.

130
Odeon Children's Circle
H.W.MILLER LTD
B'HAM 18

131
Robert Horton Fan Club
Star of the TV Western, 'Wagon Train'.

132
V Toujours Fidèle
Always faithful – a badge made in the form of a wreath for the silent-screen star Rudolph Valentino.

133
Star Cinemas Young Citizens Saturday Matinée Club
B'HAM
MEDAL BADGE CO LTD

134
Sunday Referee Shirley Temple League
RODEN LONDON
Founded in 1936, only to fold at the outset of the war, the child star's league was nevertheless highly successful during its short life.

135
Untitled
FELIX REG DESIGN 703924
MADE IN ENGLAND
The badge's design and Reg. No. suggest that

it may also have been issued as a song-title badge.

136
Untitled
PATHE PRESENTS FELIX THE CAT IN EVERYBODY'S FILM REVIEW MADE IN ENGLAND

137
Untitled
PATHE PRESENTS FELIX THE CAT IN EVERYBODY'S FILM REVIEW MADE IN ENGLAND

138
Untitled
PRO PAT
Felix's head moves to and fro.

139
Untitled
STIRLING SILVER
Includes the maker's marks of Charles Horner.

140
Untitled
STIRLING SILVER
Felix, sporting blue eyes, in a characteristic pose.

141–177 [141*]
Song Titles
In around 1924 the music publisher Laurence Wright began to produce a series of badges promoting sheet music. The badges, each produced in a variety of colourways, were sold for 9d at resorts such as Blackpool where singers accompanied by a pianist belted out the latest songs. Except for a few made by Strattons & Gaunt, the vast majority of the badges were made by Miller. Some badges have no visible title and although they often have registration numbers, their titles can only be confirmed by inference and comparison with the published sheet music. Those illustrated here that do not have a title on them are, Yes We Have No Bananas (no. 153) and Fire Fly (no. 152 – the title is on the reverse), The Shepherd on the Hill (no. 158), How Long Has This Been Going On (no. 160) and Honeysuckle Rose (no. 165). The full list of titles is unknown. However, so far some eighty or more badges in the series have been provisionally verified.

178*
Harry Roy Club
RODEN LONDON
An affectionate caricature of the highly popular 'Roaring Twenties' bandleader.

179
Tommy Steele Fan Club
PREMIER BADGES LTD LONDON

180
National Dance Band Championships
FATTORINI & SON LTD

BRADFORD WORKS BIRMINGHAM

181
I.D.M.A. Jive
International Dance Masters' Association.

182
Untitled
STRATTON BIRMINGHAM COPYRIGHT
A souvenir from the Highland Games.

183
Dumfries
STRATTON BIRMINGHAM COPYRIGHT
Another souvenir from the Highland Games.

184
C. E. Still Upward
The League of Christian Endeavour was established in 1896.

185
Salvation Army
STIRLING SILVER

186
Performing & Captive Animals Defence League Jack London Club
DESIGNED BY MARCUS STONE MEMBER OF LEAGUE DROWNED AUG 3 1931

187
Presented by the Sunday School Union For Exceptional Attendance

188
Pilots C.U. & L.M.S.
The Christian Union and London Missionary Society. 'Pilots' were members of the mission who would 'pilot' others through life.

189
Untitled
I PROMISE TO ABSTAIN FROM ALL INTOXICATING DRINKS AS BEVERAGES
Mid-19th-century temperance medal.

190*
Royal Naval Exhibition 1891

191
Souvenir de L'Exposition 1900
The Paris exhibition brought Art Nouveau to a wider public audience.

192
International Fire Exhibition 1903 Old Welcome Club
The particularly crisp die means that the fireman stands out in sharp relief.

193
Wembley Empire Exhibition 1924

194
Wembley
An unusual glass-domed badge.

195
National Dairy and Ice Cream Convention Olympia 1932
THOMAS FATTORINI LTD BIRMINGHAM
The pitted surface of the yellow enamel lends a milk pudding-like appearance to the badge's motif.

196–203
Festival of Britain 1951
Various makers.
This group of badges features the festival logo designed by Abram Games that came to epitomize British design in the 1950s.

204
Walsall General Hospital
VAUGHTONS
Hallmarked silver, 1932.

205
Young Helpers' League
A portrait of Dr Barnado, the league's renowned founder.

206
Roumanian Day
Flag day enamel badges are uncommon – they are more often printed paper pins.

207
Untitled
Stoke on Trent Children's Home, Rhyl.

237
National Asylum
Workers' Union
FATTORINI & SONS
BRADFORD
In 1918, four years
after the union had been
formed, six nurses were
denied the right to wear
this badge while on
duty. They were told that
patients were potentially in
danger of being scratched
by the badges, which
precipitated a strike.
The union amalgamated
in 1930.

238
The United 'Machine'
Glass Bottle Makers
Society
FATTORINI & SONS
BRADFORD
The society was formed
in 1918 and amalgamated
in 1925.

239
Hackney & Kingsland
Costers & Traders
Union
G. SIMMONDS LONDON

240
Liverpool Coopers
Society
REG 638232

241
Wigan & District
Weavers, Winders,
etc., Association
1913–1972.

242
Amalgamated Union of
Operative Bakers and
Confectioners

243
Organ Builders Trade
Society
c. 1879–1918.

244
Electrical Trades Union
FATTORINI & SONS LTD
BRADFORD WORKS
BIRMINGHAM
c. 1889–1968.

245
Amalgamated
Managers & Foremen's
Association
W.O. LEWIS HOWARD ST
BIRMINGHAM
c. 1917–1927.

246
National Union of
Blastfurnace Men
O.M.C.W. & K.T.
SOUVENIR MFG CO BIRM
Ore, Miners, Coke
Workers and Kindred
Trades; c. 1921–1985.

247*
National Tile, Faience
& Mosaic Fixers
Society
c. 1928–1977.

248
National Federation
of Women Workers
c. 1906–1920.

249
National Union of
Sheet Metal Workers
& Braziers

250
United Builders
Labourers Union
MANISON & CLOVER BIRM
c. 1889–1920.

251
Steam Engine Makers
Society
THOMAS FATTORINI BOLTON
c. 1826–1920.

252
Operative Bleachers,
Dyers & Finishers
Association
FATTORINI BOLTON
c. 1866–1936.

253
N.U.D.R. & G.W.
FATTORINI & SONS LTD
BRADFORD WORKS
BIRMINGHAM
A quarterly dues badge
of the National Union of
Dock Riverside & General
Workers. The origins of
this union are a little
hazy, but it had ceased
functioning by 1922.

254
N.A.S. & F.U.
SMITH & WRIGHT LTD BIRM
National Amalgamated
Sailors & Firemans Union
(c. 1887–1893). Third
quarter 'paid up dues'
badge.

255
National
Amalgamated Union
of Shop Assistants,
Warehousemen
and Clerks
1898–1947.

256
N.A.U.S.A.W. & C.
This badge, and its
companion above, display
elements of the exotic
motifs and cursive forms
particular to Art Nouveau.

257
United Operative
Plumbers &
Domestic Engineers
Association of
Great Britain & Ireland
c. 1911–1931.

258
Winsford Saltmakers
Association
FATTORINI & SONS
BRADFORD WORKS BIRM
c. 1853–1969.

259
National Union of
Agricultural & Allied
Workers
BRAVINGTONS
KING'S CROSS LONDON
c. 1968–1981.

260
N.U.A.W. County
Roadmen's Section
BRAVINGTONS
KING'S CROSS LONDON
National Union of
Agricultural Workers.

261
NU Water Works
Employees
Founded in c. 1906.

262
Guild of Sommeliers
A wine waiter's badge,
displaying an appropriately
bucolic motif.

263
Union of Public
Employees
The maker's name is
partially obscured.

264
Navvies Union
FATTORINI & SONS
BRADFORD

265
National Society
of Pottery Workers
J.R.GAUNT LONDON
c. 1917–1971.

266
Plombiers, Couvreurs
et Similaires CGT
COLOMBO
64 RUE DE LA FOLIE
MERICOURT PARIS
Plumbers, slaters, etc.,
French trade union.

267
Chemical Workers
Union
c. 1936–1971.

268
A.M.U.
FATTORINI BIRM
REG 038232
Amalgamated Musicians'
Union, c. 1884–1921.

269*
Hull City

270*
Airdrieonians
Another badge in the
same series as no. 269.

271
M. Area F.S.A.
An old Manchester Area
Football Supporter's
Association badge.

272
Voetbal 1896
A modernist badge for
the Dutch football team
Wilhelm the Second.

273
The Football
Association 1959
A Victorian-style badge.

274
Wembley 1925
Sheffield United beat
Cardiff City.

275
Aldershot Town
Supporters Club
H.W.MILLER LTD BRANSTON
ST B'HAM 18

276
Bath City A.F.
Supporters Club
MALLORY BATH

277
Bradford Northern
R.L.F. Club
FATTORINI & SONS
BRADFORD WORKS
BIRMINGHAM

278
Coventry Rugby
Supporters Club
H.W.MILLER

279
Sportsmen's
Association
Denis Compton
President 1948
Renowned test cricketer,
who never had a hair out
of place.

280
Untitled
Supporter's badge.

281
Glamorgan County
Cricket Supporters
Club

282
East Molesey Cricket
Club
FATTORINI & SONS LTD
35 BARR ST BIRM
Some delightful Victorian
colouring adorns this
badge.

283
Cricket
THOMAS FATTORINI REGENT
ST BIRMINGHAM
Similar badges exist
which denote a wide
variety of social and
cultural activities.

284
England
MILLER
118 BRANSTON ST B'HAM
Almost certainly intended
to be worn during a
test match.

285
Untitled
Like on some football
badges you can get
different team strips
on identical dies.

286
H. Greyhounds
CAXTON NAMEPLATE CO
WESTMINSTER LONDON
Harringay Ice Hockey
Club, 'The Greyhounds'.

287
Untitled
STRATTONS ENGLAND
Unidentified strips.

288
Hull Roller Skating
Club

289
Brighton & Hove
Ice Rink
THOMAS FATTORINI LTD
BIRMINGHAM

290
Brough Park
Racing Club
REID & SONS LTD
NEWCASTLE ON TYNE
Greyhound racing was
introduced in Britain
in 1926.

291
Untitled
A high-quality generic
badge.

292
Untitled
Souvenir of a Scottish
golf tournament.

293
Untitled
Unidentified comic
character.

294*
Untitled
Figural badges, such as
this one, are a genre in
themselves.

295
Horsforth Golf Club
W.S.D.
Silver hallmarks for 1924.

296
Bothwell Castle Golf
Club

297
Untitled
This elegantly made set of
golf clubs has a brooch-
like quality.

298
Dunlop
CASHMORE & CO BIRM
A popular promotional
image of the 1930s.

299
Felixstowe Golf Club

300
Kempton Park Club
1894
Horse racing entry badges
were first introduced
at the Doncaster races
in 1820 when silver
badges were sold to
raise a subscription
fund to erect a stand.

301
Olympiska Spelen
Stockholm 1912
Silver hallmarks.

302
1935
J.R.GAUNT LONDON
Commemorating the
lighting of the Olympic
torch for the 1936 games
in Berlin.

303
XI. Olympiade Berlin
1936
W.D. GES. GESCH.

304
Neuchâtel Lawn Tennis
Silver membership badge
for the Neuchâtel Lawn
Tennis Club, located to
the North of Lake Geneva
(c. 1900).

305
Little Common
Tennis Club
T.F. HOCKLEY ST BIRM
Sussex village near
Brighton.

306
C. W. Staniforth
Bowling Club
CO-OP WOMEN'S
Bowling badges often
have views of their
particular locality.
This building is probably
the local headquarters of
the Co-op.

LIST OF ILLUSTRATIONS

341*
ZIP Guaranteed Oils
THOMAS FATTORINI LTD
REGENT ST BIRMINGHAM
ZIP was the trade name of
an aviation fuel exported
to Britain by 'Russian Oil
Products' during the
1930s.

342
Amy's Jason
STRATTON & CO
BIRMINGHAM COPYRIGHT
A celebration of Amy
Johnson's pioneering
solo flight in 1930 to
Australia in her aeroplane
Jason. See no. 172, the
'Amy' badge.

343
National League of
Airmen 1935
RODEN LONDON

344
Untitled
A Douglas D.C.2. pin.

345
Hindenburg
The airship travelled
extensively between
Germany and America. It
caught fire in 1937 while
landing at New Jersey
with tragic loss of life.

346
Butlin's Camp
Skegness 1939
HOLIDAYS ARE JOLLYDAYS
In December 1936, just
in time for Christmas,
Billy Butlin opened his
first holiday camp at
Skegness – the camp's

badge took the form of
a decorated tree. In 1937
the company took the
motif of the jolly fisherman
from a poster designed by
John Hassall for the N. E.
Railway's promotion of
Skegness and began
incorporating it into much
of the camp's publicity.

347
Butlin's Filey 1945
HOLIDAYS ARE JOLLYDAYS
The Filey camp was
built for the RAF in 1939.
Billy Butlin must have
had confidence in the
outcome of the war as he
had inserted a clause into
the contract which entitled
him to buy back the
camp on highly favourable
terms when the hostilities
ceased. The badge, with
its 'V' sign, was not widely
circulated due to the
camp's hurried opening
in time for Christmas.

348
Butlin's
Skegness 1948
During the war the camp
was occupied by the navy
and for security reasons
called HMS Arthur and
placed on the admiralty
list. This led to a hilarious
episode when the
traitor Lord Haw Haw,
broadcasting out of Berlin,
announced that HMS
Arthur had sunk during
a naval engagement.
The camp was still fitted
out and decorated for
holiday makers when

able seaman George
Melly was stationed
there. He recounts in his
autobiography, Rum Bum
and Baccy, that he was
pleasantly surprised to
discover that the navy
had decorated the
camp in the style of
the Surrealists. Melly was
particularly impressed with
the décor of the medical
room – a pirates' cave
resplendent in papier
maché walls, resembling
rock formations, which
were dotted with papier
maché skeletons.

349
Butlin's
Skegness 1953

350
Butlin's
Filey 1950
FATTORINI & SONS LTD
BRADFORD WORKS
BIRMINGHAM

351
Butlin's
Filey 1955

352
Butlin's
Skegness 1955
J.R.GAUNT LONDON
As with many of Butlin's
badges, this design
was made in a variety
of colourways and in
different formats. Wearing
a 'current' badge meant
staff could identify you
as a bona fide camper.

353
Grand Bahama Club
FATTORINI & SONS LTD
BAAR ST. B'HAM. ENG.
Butlin's opened two 'up
market' hotels in the
Bahamas in 1949 – the
Grand Bahama Club and
the Fort Montague Beach
Club at Nassau. Within
six months the camps
had closed due to a lack
of business.

354
Butlin's Margate 1958

355
Butlin's Clacton 1946
Female bathers at Butlin's
appear to have stolen
the march on the fashion
for bikinis. Bikinis were
named after the Pacific
atoll where the atomic
tests were held in 1949.

356
Butlin's Ayr 1952
FATTORINI & SONS
BRADFORD WORKS
BIRMINGHAM
The camp opened
in 1947, having been
used by the military
during the war.

357
Butlin's Clacton 1939
BERNARD FRENCH
39 STATION ROAD
CLACTON-ON-SEA
During the first few
months of the war the
camp was employed as
an internment camp for
German civilians. Later it
was used by the pioneer

corps for the remainder
of the war.

358
Butlin's Ireland 1956
This is the only badge
that features a Butlin's
Redcoat. The details
are transfer printed.

359
Butlin's Brighton 1962
J.R.GAUNT LONDON
During the 1960s
Gaunt's designs for
Butlin's badges appear
to have been much more
influenced by minimalism.

360
Butlin's Bognor 1960
W.REEVES & CO LTD
BIRMINGHAM

361
Butlin's Minehead
1967
MORTON COLVER 1967361

362
Hurrah! It's Butlin's

363
Untitled
Awarded as a prize in
a sandcastle-building
competition.

364
Butlin's Pwllheli 1955
This camp, like others,
was due to open in
1939, but was taken over
for naval duties at the
outbreak of war. It was
decommissioned in 1947.

169

401*
Late R.M.S. Titanic
April 15th 1912
C.C. REGD

402
R.M.S. Carpathia
Launched in 1902,
the Carpathia rescued the
survivors from the Titanic,
but was herself torpedoed
in 1918. Her own
survivors were rescued
by H.M.S. Snowdrop.

403
R.M.S. Ophir
B BROS.
Silver hallmarked, c.1910.

404
R.M.S. Newfoundland
A non-enamelled badge
transfer printed over
butterfly wings and
encased under glass.

405
R.M.S. Ivernia
REG 364020
A liner of the White Star
Line.

406
Normandie
DUSEAUX.
29 R' PASTOURELLE PARIS
A French Trans-Atlantic
liner.

407–418
Various
A flotilla of voyage-
souvenir and fund-
raising railway orphanage
badges, mostly made by
Miller & Stratton.

419
Lifeboat Saturday
1908
REG NO 518810
The Lifeboat Service was
established in 1824. Its
president, the Prince of
Wales, later King George
V, formed the Lifeboat
Fund in 1899.

420
Collector
J.R.GAUNT & CO LTD
LONDON
Like the previous two
badges, a 'Collector'
badge could only be worn
by an official Flag Day
Fund Collector.

421
Hull Fish Dock
Workers
W.O.LEWIS BADGES LTD
BIRMINGHAM
The button-hole fitting has
been designed to fit easily
into overalls.

422
Untitled
A Grimsby Steam Fishing
Vessels Engineers &
Firemans Union
trawlerman's trunk badge.

423
Syndicat des Ouvriers
de la Companie
du Canal de Suez.
Port Said 1919
SAF 122 FIRENZE.
An unusual French trade
union badge worn by
the builders of the Suez
Canal

424
National Amalgamated
Society of Operative
House & Ship Painters
& Decorators
FATTORONI BRADFORD

425
N.A.S. & D. Dockers
Section
W.O. LEWIS BADGES
LTD BIRMINGHAM
National Amalgamated
Stevedores & Dockers
Union (c. 1931–1982).

426
N.U.S. Annual General
Meeting London 1931
The union ran from 1926
to 1993.

427
National Union of
General & Municipal
Workers
Fish Bobber 1
FRANK COBB & CO LTD
SHEFFIELD
Bobbers transferred
the catch from the
quayside to the daily
fish auction.

428
N.U. of D.L.
National Union of Dock
Labourers (c. 1889–
1992). Quarterly dues
badges were produced
in a variety of distinctively
shaped dies.

429
British Seafarers Union
FATTORINI BRADFORD
The union was in

existence between
1911 and 1922.

430
Hull Seamens Union
1881 N.T.W.F.
W. EVETTS. BIRM
The initials stand for
National Transport
Workers Federation.

431
Ship Constructors
& Shipwrights
Association
The trade union was in
existence between 1910
and 1963 – note the
ship's name!

432
Chevrolet
WM MILLER
118 BRANSTON ST B'HAM

433
Rover
H.W.MILLER
118 BRANSTON ST B'HAM

434
Riley Motor Club
B'HAM MEDAL & BADGES
CO LTD. ALBION ST
BIRMINGHAM

435
Lagonda Staines
England
Salesman's badge.

436
Triumph
WM MILLER
118 BRANSTON ST
BIRMINGHAM
MADE IN ENGLAND

437
Minerva
A Belgian motor car
manufacturer.

438
Vauxhall Engineering
H.W.MILLER LTD

439
Goodyear Tyres

440
Hotchkiss Paris
Salon 1931

441
Avon
WM MILLER
118 BRANSTON ST
BIRMINGHAM
A tyre manufacturer.

442
Dunlop 1888–1938
G MORET
79 FG DU TEMPLE PARIS

443
Castrol
BUTLER BIRMINGHAM

444
Jaguar Coventry

445
Jowett Cars Limited
FATTORINI BRADFORD

446
Fiat
S.JOHNSON MILAN

An unusual sweetheart badge which is painted rather than enamelled.

543
St Pancras Bomber Club

544
Submarine Service
SILVER

545
Deutschland
Probably commemorating the German submarine's visit to America in 1916.

546
H.M.S. Fame
REGD
Silver hallmarks.

547
Untitled
A sweetheart badge.

548
Untitled
This polished steel sweetheart badge was probably made in a naval engineering workshop.

549
The National Sweet Pea Society
FATTORINI & SONS
35 BARR ST BIRM

550
Gardeners Institute
This richly coloured badge displays an extremely early registration number on its face.

551
English Draughts Association

552
Small Pig Keepers' Council

553
The National English Rabbit Club
FATTORINI & SONS
BRADFORD WORKS
BIRMINGHAM

554
Western Horsemen's Association of Great Britain

555
Brown & Polson Cookery Club
RODEN LONDON

556
Great Dane Breeders Association

557
It's Mine, I Saw It First
Refers to the acrimonious dispute in 1909 between Admiral F. Peary and Frederick Cook over which of them had reached the North Pole first.

558
Monmouthshire Mining Students' Association
A transfer-printed and hand-enamelled badge.

559
BORO Good Luck
H.W.M.

560
Untitled

561
Untitled
STRATTONS
MADE IN ENGLAND
Another version of this badge has H.M.S. *Valient* on a scroll added to its base.

562
Untitled

563
Untitled
MILLER
118 BRANSTON ST B'HAM
Pillar Box Club.

564
Untitled
W.MILLER
118 BRANSTON ST B'HAM
REG APPD

565
Untitled
MILLER
118 BRANSTON ST B'HAM
A memento of a visit to Santa's grotto at Selfridges.

566
Selfridges
W.MILLER
118 BRANSTON ST B'HAM
REG APPD
See badge no. 565.

567
Untitled
An exotic mixture of rhinestones and mother of pearl adorn this rather brooch-like badge. Possibly an early Selfridges issue.

568
Bureau of Freelance Photographers

569
Untitled

570
United Kingdom Atomic Energy Authority

571
Safety First
H.W.MILLER LTD BRANSTON ST BIRMINGHAM 18
REG 800096
In 1934 the then Minister of Transport Leslie Hore Belisha introduced traffic beacons to British roadsides, as well as the 30 mph speed limit.

572
Tarzan Club
TWEER & TURCK
LÜDENSCHEID
This rare German button badge is indicative of the wide dissemination of American popular culture in pre-war Europe. Button badges as we know them today were first patented in 1896 by Whitehead and Hoag of Newark, New Jersey, the same year that

another important use for celluloid was discovered – nitrate film.

573
Untitled
Lithographed directly on to tin, this Popeye badge may have been distributed as a promotional premium.

574*
Untitled
A ceramic badge of a moth – probably sold to raise funds for the 'Winterhilfswerk' (a winter relief fund) during the Third Reich.

Badge Clubs

Badge Collectors' Circle,
3 Ellis Close, Quorn,
Loughborough, LE12 HS8.

Brewery Badge Collectors' Circle,
50 Lime Grove, Stapleford,
Nottingham, NG9 7GF.

Trade Union Collectors' Club,
82 Urmston Lane,
Manchester, M32 PBQ.

Badge Auctioneers

J&B Croucher,
3 Adur Avenue,
Shoreham-by-Sea,
West Sussex, BN43 5NN.

Hakes Americana,
PO Box 444, York,
PA 17405, U.S.A.

Key Badge Collections

British Museum,
Great Russell Street,
London, WC1B 3DG.
*Pilgrim badges (Department of Medieval
Studies) and various badges (Department of
Coins and Medals).*

The Museum of London,
London Wall,
London, EC2Y 5HN.
Pilgrim badges (Medieval Department).

National Museum of Labour History,
The Pump House,
People's History Museum,
Left Bank,
Bridge Street,
Manchester, M3 3ER.
Trade Union and political badges.